# Introduction

Sticky Maths Primary offers more than just math's. It provides a way to build a learning paradigm to develop other math's concepts through interactive lessons, exercises and quizzes. The whole content is created by a qualified math's teacher that you can trust and look up for any guidance.

Sticky Maths Primary has everything that a 4th grade student needs to learn. It is suitable for ages 5 to 12 and incredibly helpful in building a level of mathematical fluency before SATs, 11+ or even starting secondary school.

Sticky Maths Primary workbook includes various questions for crucial primary school topics, suggestions, and tips to deal with easily forgotten concepts. Answers have also been included. This all-inclusive math's workbook is one of the most helpful resources for a struggling child to proceed in the following grades confidently.

# Dedication

Dedicated to:

Michelle Ayomikun: my Pride and my Joy

And my parents: Biodun and Bisi, whose prayers keep me going.

# Table of Contents

## Chapter 6

# Chapter 1

# Part A: 1, 2 and 3 Times table

### 1) Multiplication

1 x 1 =

2 x 1 =

3 x 1 =

4 x 1 =

5 x 1 =

6 x 1 =

7 x 1 =

8 x 1 =

9 x 1 =

10 x 1 =

11 x 1 =

12 x 1 =

### 2) Division

9 ÷ 1 =

5 ÷ 1 =

1 ÷ 1 =

10 ÷ 1 =

6 ÷ 1 =

2 ÷ 1 =

11 ÷ 1 =

7 ÷ 1 =

3 ÷ 1 =

12 ÷ 1 =

8 ÷ 1 =

4 ÷ 1 =

**Tip:** Sing the 2 times table song when doing this exercise.

### 3) Multiplication

1 x 2 =

2 x 2 =

3 x 2 =

4 x 2 =

5 x 2 =

6 x 2 =

7 x 2 =

8 x 2 =

9 x 2 =

10 x 2 =

11 x 2 =

12 x 2 =

### 4) Division

18 ÷ 2 =

10 ÷ 2 =

2 ÷ 2 =

20 ÷ 2 =

12 ÷ 2 =

4 ÷ 2 =

22 ÷ 2 =

14 ÷ 2 =

6 ÷ 2 =

24 ÷ 2 =

16 ÷ 2 =

8 ÷ 2 =

Do you need help with the division exercise? Remember  7 x 2 = 14
So what will  14 ÷ 2 be? Yes, that's right. It's 7!

Now your turn
        24 x 12 = 24
        5) 24 ÷ 2 =  _____

 **Tip:** Sing the 3 times table song when doing this exercise.

| 6) Multiplication | | 7) Division | |
|---|---|---|---|
| 1 x 3 = | ☐ | 27 ÷ 3 = | ☐ |
| 2 x 3 = | ☐ | 15 ÷ 3 = | ☐ |
| 3 x 3 = | ☐ | 3 ÷ 3 = | ☐ |
| 4 x 3 = | ☐ | 30 ÷ 3 = | ☐ |
| 5 x 3 = | ☐ | 18 ÷ 3 = | ☐ |
| 6 x 3 = | ☐ | 6 ÷ 3 = | ☐ |
| 7 x 3 = | ☐ | 33 ÷ 3 = | ☐ |
| 8 x 3 = | ☐ | 21 ÷ 3 = | ☐ |
| 9 x 3 = | ☐ | 9 ÷ 3 = | ☐ |
| 10 x 3 = | ☐ | 36 ÷ 3 = | ☐ |
| 11 x 3 = | ☐ | 24 ÷ 3 = | ☐ |
| 12 x 3 = | ☐ | 12 ÷ 3 = | ☐ |

Do you need help with the division exercise?
**Remember 5 x 3 = 15 Therefore 15 ÷ 3 will**
be _____?
Yes that's right 5!

**Now your turn**
9 x 3 = 27
8) 27 ÷ 3 =  _____

And another one

10 x 3 = 30

9) 30 ÷ 3 = _____

10) Can you explain what is going on here?

_____

_____

_____

11) Fill in the missing numbers.

2 ___ 6 ___ ___ 12 ___ 16 ___ 20 ____ ____

3 ___ 9 ___ ___ 18 ___ 24 ___ 30 ____ 36

12) Challenge: Mixed questions

2 x 3 = ☐

4 x 2 = ☐

6 x 3 = ☐

5 x 2 = ☐

8 x 3 = ☐

2 x 1 = ☐

9 x 3 = ☐

# Part B: Factors

What are factors?

Factors are **legs**. Yes, LEGS!

To find the factors of 8, look for two numbers you can multiply to give 8.

**Tip:** Start with 1 and the number. In this case, that will be 1 and **8**.

Then find the other numbers. That will be **2** and **4**.

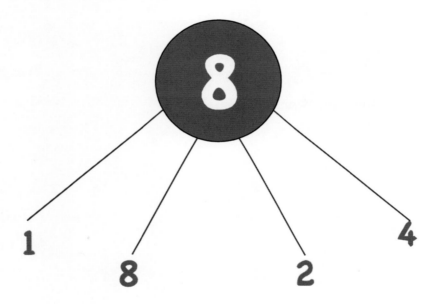

The factors of 8 are: 1, 8, 2 and 4

Do you see what I mean by factors? Are you ready to try some exercises?

Here are your own circles. Now draw the legs!!!

**4**

1) The factors of 4 are _____

Don't forget to draw the legs!

**6**

2) The factors of 6 are _____

Don't forget to draw the legs!

**Tip:** Some numbers have more than 4 factors. To get 12, you can multiply 1 x 12, 2 x 6 and 3 x 4.

Now draw the legs! How many are there?

3) The factors of 12 are _____

Don't forget to draw the legs!

4) The factors of 18 _____

Don't forget to draw the legs!

5) Which of the following numbers are NOT factors of 36? Circle them.

1   2   3   5   6   7   8   9   12   18   38

6) Fill in the missing factors of 21.

_____ 3 _____ 21

7) Circle the common factors of 12 and 18.

12:   1   12   2   6   3   4

18:   1   18   3   6   2   9

8) Now, out of all the common factors you circled, which one is the Highest Common Factor?

_____

# Part C: Multiples

We learnt a rhyme for multiples in the Primary Maths Program (PMP) online course. Do you remember?

**1) Complete the rhyme.**

**Tip: The rhyme goes like this:**

Multiples mean multiply Times what?
Times table

This means that the multiples of 3 are the numbers in the 3 times table: 3 6 9 12 15. . . and so on.

The multiples of 2 are the numbers in the 2 times table: 2 4 6 8 10 12. . . and so on.

**2)** List the first 5 multiples of 1.

_____

**3)** List the first 7 multiples of 2.

_____

**4)** List the first 8 multiples of 3.

_____

**5) Here's a slightly tricky one but I know you will give it a try. List the first 5 multiples of 10.**

_____

# Part D: Prime numbers

We learnt the prime number song in the Primary Maths Program (PMP) online course. Do you remember?

1) Complete this prime number song:

2 _____ 5 _____ 11 _____

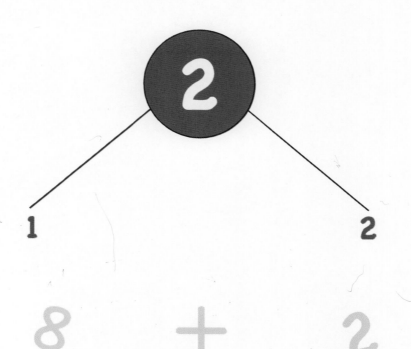

**Tip:** The song goes like this:

2   3   5   7   11   13

Every prime number has the same number of legs as you?

2) How many legs do prime numbers have? _____

Do you remember what "legs" are?

3) Legs are _____
(Revisit part B of Chapter 1 to recall what we said legs are)

Prime numbers have 2 factors.

2 is a prime number because it only has 2 factors: 1 and 2. Remember: A prime number is a  number that can only be divided by itself and 1.

4) Is 15 a prime number?    YES    NO

 **Tip:** A number that has <u>more</u> than 2 factors is not a prime number. A prime number has **only 2 factors (legs).**

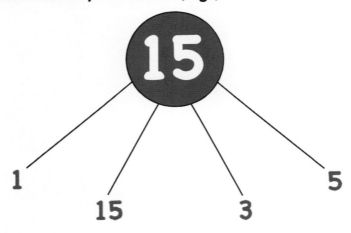

5) Is 17 a prime number?    YES    NO

(don't forget to draw legs on 17 before you decide on Yes or No)

**Complete the legs to find answer.**

6) What are the prime numbers between 1 and 20?

_____

7) Challenge yourself! What are the prime numbers between 20 and 30?

_____

8). How many of the prime numbers in Question 6 above are also even numbers?

_____

9) All prime numbers are odd numbers.     YES     NO
Can you explain why?

_____

10) Is 1 a prime number?     YES     NO

Can you explain why? _____

1

# Chapter 2:

# Part A: 4, 5 and 6 Times table

 **Tip:** Sing the 4 times table song when doing this exercise..

**1) Multiplication**

1 x 4 =

2 x 4 =

3 x 4 =

4 x 4 =

5 x 4 =

6 x 4 =

7 x 4 =

8 x 4 =

9 x 4 =

10 x 4 =

11 x 4 =

12 x 4 =

**2) Division**

36 ÷ 4 =

20 ÷ 4 =

4 ÷ 4 =

40 ÷ 4 =

24 ÷ 4 =

8 ÷ 4 =

44 ÷ 4 =

28 ÷ 4 =

12 ÷ 4 =

48 ÷ 4 =

32 ÷ 4 =

16 ÷ 4 =

Do you need help with the division exercise?

Remember: 3 x 4 = 12
Then 12 ÷ 4 will be _____?
Yes that's right 3!

Now your turn
7 x 4 = 28
3) 28 ÷ 4 = _____

One more
12 x 4 = 48
4) 48 ÷ 4 = _____

5) Can you explain what is going on here?

_____
_____
_____

6) Fill in the missing numbers.

4 ___ 12 ___ ___ 24 ___ 32 ___ 40 ___ ___

___ 8 ___ ___ 20 ___ 28 ___ 36 ___ 44 ___

7) Challenge: Mixed questions

10 x 4 = ☐
4 x 4 = ☐
6 x 4 = ☐
3 x 4 = ☐
8 x 4 = ☐
3 x 4 = ☐
9 x 4 = ☐

8) Multiplication

1 x 5 = ☐
2 x 5 = ☐
3 x 5 = ☐
4 x 5 = ☐
5 x 5 = ☐
6 x 5 = ☐
7 x 5 = ☐
8 x 5 = ☐
9 x 5 = ☐
10 x 5 = ☐
11 x 5 = ☐
12 x 5 = ☐

9) Division

45 ÷ 5 = ☐
25 ÷ 5 = ☐
5 ÷ 5 = ☐
50 ÷ 5 = ☐
30 ÷ 5 = ☐
10 ÷ 5 = ☐
55 ÷ 5 = ☐
35 ÷ 5 = ☐
15 ÷ 5 = ☐
60 ÷ 5 = ☐
40 ÷ 5 = ☐
20 ÷ 5 = ☐

Do you need help with the division exercise?

Remember: **8 x 5 = 40**
So what will **40 ÷ 5** be?
Yes, that's right. It's **8**!

Now your turn 4 x 5 = 20
10) 20 ÷ 5 = _____

One more
6 x 5 = 30
11) 30 ÷ 5 = _____

12) Can you explain what is going on here?

_____

_____

_____

13) Fill in the missing numbers.

5__ 15 ____ ____ 30 ____ 40 ____ 50 _____ _____

____ 10 ____ ____ 25 ____ 35 ____ 45 _____ 55 _____

14) Challenge: Mixed questions

9 x 5  =  ☐
4 x 5  =  ☐
6 x 5  =  ☐
3 x 5  =  ☐
8 x 5  =  ☐
2 x 5  =  ☐
9 x 5  =  ☐

**Tip:** Sing the 6 times table song when doing this exercise.

### 15) Multiplication

1 x 6 = [ ]

2 x 6 = [ ]

3 x 6 = [ ]

4 x 6 = [ ]

5 x 6 = [ ]

6 x 6 = [ ]

7 x 6 = [ ]

8 x 6 = [ ]

9 x 6 = [ ]

10 x 6 = [ ]

11 x 6 = [ ]

12 x 6 = [ ]

### 16) Division

54 ÷ 6 = [ ]

30 ÷ 6 = [ ]

6 ÷ 6 = [ ]

60 ÷ 6 = [ ]

36 ÷ 6 = [ ]

12 ÷ 6 = [ ]

66 ÷ 6 = [ ]

42 ÷ 6 = [ ]

18 ÷ 6 = [ ]

72 ÷ 6 = [ ]

48 ÷ 6 = [ ]

24 ÷ 6 = [ ]

Do you need help with the division exercise?

Remember: 3 x 6 = 18
So what will 18 ÷ 6 be?
Yes, that's right. It's 3!

Now your turn
7 x 6 = 42
17) 42 ÷ 6 = _____

One more 12 x 6 = 72
18) 72 ÷ 6 = _____

19) Can you explain what is going on here?

_____

_____

**20) Fill in the missing numbers**

6 ___ 18 ___ ___ 36 ___ 48 ___ 60 ____ ____

___ 12 ___ ___ 30 ___ 42 ___ 54 ____ 66 ____

**21) Challenge: Mixed questions**

**Remember:** Sing the 6 times table song if you need help.

| | | | |
|---|---|---|---|
| $10 \times 6 =$ ☐ | $30 \div 6 =$ ☐ | $42 \div 6 =$ ☐ |
| $4 \times 6 =$ ☐ | $12 \div 6 =$ ☐ | $18 \div 6 =$ ☐ |
| $6 \times 6 =$ ☐ | $42 \div 6 =$ ☐ | $6 \div 6 =$ ☐ |
| $3 \times 6 =$ ☐ | $24 \div 6 =$ ☐ | $36 \div 6 =$ ☐ |
| $8 \times 6 =$ ☐ | $54 \div 6 =$ ☐ | $72 \div 6 =$ ☐ |
| $2 \times 6 =$ ☐ | $66 \div 6 =$ ☐ | $66 \div 6 =$ ☐ |
| $9 \times 6 =$ ☐ | $6 \div 6 =$ ☐ | $48 \div 6 =$ ☐ |

## 22) More challenges: Short Multiplcation

Oh dear, Miss Tutu. What are you doing giving us all of these big challenges?

Miss Tutu says, "Keep going. You've got this!"

See an example below:

$$
\begin{array}{r}
{}^{+1}2 \quad 4 \\
\times \quad 3 \\
\hline
7 \quad 2
\end{array}
$$

Carry Stays
↓    ↓
3 × 4 = 1 2

a)  $\begin{array}{r} 1\ 9 \\ \times\ 6 \\ \hline \end{array}$

b)  $\begin{array}{r} 1\ 5 \\ \times\ 6 \\ \hline \end{array}$

c)  $\begin{array}{r} 1\ 7 \\ \times\ 6 \\ \hline \end{array}$

d)  $\begin{array}{r} 1\ 8 \\ \times\ 6 \\ \hline \end{array}$

e)  $\begin{array}{r} 1\ 4 \\ \times\ 6 \\ \hline \end{array}$

# Part B: Short division

Solve.

 **Tip: If you don't remember how, rewatch the video on short divisions in the PMP online course.**

$$6 \overline{)5^5 2^4 8} \quad\begin{array}{c} 0\,8\,8 \end{array}$$

Remainder = 52-48=4

1) $5\overline{)90}$

3) $5\overline{)405}$

5) $3\overline{)165}$

2) $4\overline{)192}$

4) $3\overline{)90}$

6) $3\overline{)246}$

# Chapter 3
# Part A: 7 and 8 Times table

 Tip: Sing the 7 times table song when doing this exercise.

**1) Multiplication**

| | | |
|---|---|---|
| 1 x 7 | = | ☐ |
| 2 x 7 | = | ☐ |
| 3 x 7 | = | ☐ |
| 4 x 7 | = | ☐ |
| 5 x 7 | = | ☐ |
| 6 x 7 | = | ☐ |
| 7 x 7 | = | ☐ |
| 8 x 7 | = | ☐ |
| 9 x 7 | = | ☐ |
| 10 x 7 | = | ☐ |
| 11 x 7 | = | ☐ |
| 12 x 7 | = | ☐ |

**2) Division**

| | | |
|---|---|---|
| 63 ÷ 7 | = | ☐ |
| 35 ÷ 7 | = | ☐ |
| 7 ÷ 7 | = | ☐ |
| 70 ÷ 7 | = | ☐ |
| 42 ÷ 7 | = | ☐ |
| 14 ÷ 7 | = | ☐ |
| 77 ÷ 7 | = | ☐ |
| 49 ÷ 7 | = | ☐ |
| 21 ÷ 7 | = | ☐ |
| 84 ÷ 7 | = | ☐ |
| 56 ÷ 7 | = | ☐ |
| 28 ÷ 7 | = | ☐ |

Do you need help with the division exercise?

Remember: 4 x 7 = 28
So what will 28 ÷ 7 be?
Yes, that's right. It's 4!

Now your turn
9 x 7 = 63
3) 63 ÷ 7 = _____

12 x 7 = _____ (You should know this without singing as it is the last number on the 7 times table.)

4) 84 ÷ 7 = _____

Here is one more!

10 x 7 = _____

**Brainteaser:** When you multiply a number by 10, what happens?

_____

_____

5) 70 ÷ 7 = ____

6) Fill in the missing numbers

7 ___ 21 ___ ___ 42 ___ 56 ___ 70 ____ ____

___ 14 ___ ___ 35 ___ ___ ____ 63 ____ ____ ____

7) Challenge: Mixed questions

Tip: Use your fingers and lines if you need to.

10 x 7 = [ ]
4 x 7 = [ ]
6 x 7 = [ ]
3 x 7 = [ ]
8 x 7 = [ ]
2 x 7 = [ ]
11 x 7 = [ ]

(Do you really need fingers or lines for this, what happens when you times a number by 11? If you are not sure, ask an adult, it saves tons of time)

## 8) Division Challenge

Tip: Use circles for this challenge. It will make it easier.

$$28 \div 7 = ?$$

$$28 \div 7 = 4$$

$35 \div 7 =$ ☐

$14 \div 7 =$ ☐

$84 \div 7 =$ ☐

$56 \div 7 =$ ☐

$77 \div 7 =$ ☐

$84 \div 7 =$ ☐

$21 \div 7 =$ ☐

## 9) Help Miss Tutu find the wrong multiples of 7. Cross out the wrong numbers and write the correct number in the box above it.

☐ ☐ ☐ ☐ ☐ ☐ ☐ ☐ ☐ ☐ ☐ ☐

7    12    21    28    30    42    49    56    67    70    77    88

10) More challenges: Short Multiplication.

```
 +1
   2  ←      4
              ↑
   ×         3
 -------------
   7         2
```

Carry  Stays
  ↓     ↓
3 × 4 = 1 2

a)  2   2       b)  3   2       c)  4   1
    ×   7           ×   7           ×   7
   -----           -----           -----

d)  9   0       e) 8   1
    ×   7          ×   7
   -----          -----

**Tip:** Sing the 8 times table song when doing this exercise.

## 11) Multiplication

1 x 8   =   ☐

2 x 8   =   ☐

3 x 8   =   ☐

4 x 8   =   ☐

5 x 8   =   ☐

6 x 8   =   ☐

7 x 8   =   ☐

8 x 8   =   ☐

9 x 8   =   ☐

10 x 8   =   ☐

11 x 8   =   ☐

12 x 8   =   ☐

## 12) Division

72 ÷ 8   =   ☐

40 ÷ 8   =   ☐

8 ÷ 8   =   ☐

80 ÷ 8   =   ☐

48 ÷ 8   =   ☐

16 ÷ 8   =   ☐

88 ÷ 8   =   ☐

56 ÷ 8   =   ☐

24 ÷ 8   =   ☐

96 ÷ 8   =   ☐

64 ÷ 8   =   ☐

32 ÷ 8   =   ☐

## 13) Advanced Challenge: Long multiplication

carry   stays

$4 \times 5 = 2\,0$

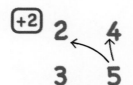

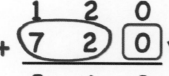

always put a place holder here

26

a)  2 2
  × 1 8
  ------

b)  3 2
  × 2 8
  ------

c)  4 1
  × 4 8
  ------

d)  9 0
  × 3 8
  ------

e)  8 1
  × 5 8
  ------

# Part B: Short division

 Tip: Quickly revise long divisions from the PMP online course before doing this exercise.

$$6 \overline{)5^5 2^4 8} \quad 088$$

Remainder = 52-48=4

Solve in your exercise book and fill in the answers.

a) $11\overline{)8\,4\,7}$

d) $4\overline{)6\,4}$

b) $3\overline{)2\,6\,1}$

e) $5\overline{)4\,3\,0}$

c) $1\overline{)9\,3}$

f) $12\overline{)5\,8\,8}$

# Chapter 4
# Part A: 9, 10 and 11 Times table

 **Tip:** Sing the 9 times table song when doing this exercise.

| 1) Multiplication | | 2) Division | |
|---|---|---|---|
| 1 x 9 = ☐ | | 81 ÷ 9 = ☐ | |
| 2 x 9 = ☐ | | 45 ÷ 9 = ☐ | |
| 3 x 9 = ☐ | | 9 ÷ 9 = ☐ | |
| 4 x 9 = ☐ | | 90 ÷ 9 = ☐ | |
| 5 x 9 = ☐ | | 54 ÷ 9 = ☐ | |
| 6 x 9 = ☐ | | 18 ÷ 9 = ☐ | |
| 7 x 9 = ☐ | | 99 ÷ 9 = ☐ | |
| 8 x 9 = ☐ | | 63 ÷ 9 = ☐ | |
| 9 x 9 = ☐ | | 27 ÷ 9 = ☐ | |
| 10 x 9 = ☐ | | 108 ÷ 9 = ☐ | |
| 11 x 9 = ☐ | | 72 ÷ 9 = ☐ | |
| 12 x 9 = ☐ | | 36 ÷ 9 = ☐ | |

Do you need help with the division exercise?

Remember: 4 x 9 = 36
So what will 36 ÷ 9 be?
Yes, that's right. It's 4!

Now your turn
9 x 8 = 72
3) 72 ÷ 9 = _____

Here is another one.

12 x 9 = _____ (You should know this without singing as it is the last number on the 9 times table.)

4) 108 ÷ 9 = _____

**Let us do one more.**

10 x 9 = _____

5) 90 ÷ 9 = _____

6) Fill in the missing numbers.

9 ___ 27 ___ ___ 54 ___ 72 ___ 90 ___ ___

___ 18 ___ ___ 45 ___ ___ ___ 81 ___ ___ ___

7) Challenge: Mixed questions

10 x 9 = ⬜

4 x 9 = ⬜

6 x 9 = ⬜

3 x 9 = ⬜

8 x 9 = ⬜

2 x 9 = ⬜

11 x 9 = ⬜

Some Division Challenge

(Use circles for this challenge, it will make it easier)

45 ÷ 9 = ⬜

18 ÷ 9 = ⬜

108 ÷ 9 = ⬜

63 ÷ 9 = ⬜

99 ÷ 9 = ⬜

27 ÷ 9 = ⬜

9 ÷ 9 = ⬜

9) More division exercises

1) 81 ÷ 9 = _____

2) 72 ÷ 9 = _____

3) 90 ÷ 9 = _____

4) 9 ÷ 9 = _____

5) 18 ÷ 9 = _____

6) 27 ÷ 9 = _____

10) Help Miss Tutu find the wrong multiples of 9. Cross out the wrong numbers and write the correct number in the box above it.

| | | | | | | | | | | | |
|---|---|---|---|---|---|---|---|---|---|---|---|
| 9 | 18 | 26 | 36 | 45 | 59 | 63 | 71 | 81 | 90 | 99 | 100 |

Tip: Do you know you do NOT need a song for the 10 times table?

11) Multiplication

1 x 10   =  [   ]

2 x 10   =  [   ]

3 x 10   =  [   ]

4 x 10   =  [   ]

5 x 10   =  [   ]

6 x 10   =  [   ]

7 x 10   =  [   ]

8 x 10   =  [   ]

9 x 10   =  [   ]

10 x 10  =  [   ]

11 x 10  =  [   ]

12 x 10  =  [   ]

12) Division

90 ÷ 10   =  [   ]

50 ÷ 10   =  [   ]

10 ÷ 10   =  [   ]

100 ÷ 10  =  [   ]

60 ÷ 10   =  [   ]

20 ÷ 10   =  [   ]

110 ÷ 10  =  [   ]

70 ÷ 10   =  [   ]

30 ÷ 10   =  [   ]

120 ÷ 10  =  [   ]

80 ÷ 10   =  [   ]

40 ÷ 10   =  [   ]

## 13) Advanced challenge: Long multiplication

carry stays
$4 \times 5 = 2\,0$

```
   +2  2      4
          3   5
       ─────────
       1  2   0
    + (7  2) [0]  ← always put a
       ─────────    place holder here
       8  4   0
```

```
   +1  2      4
              3
       ─────────
        (7   2)
```

a)  2 2
  × 1 7
  -----

b)  3 2
  × 2 7
  -----

c)  4 1
  × 4 7
  -----

d)  9 0
  × 3 7
  -----

e)  8 1
  × 5 7
  -----

29

Do you need help with the division exercise?

Remember: 11 x 9 = 99

 **Tip:** Sing the 11 times table song when doing this exercise.

### 14) Multiplication

1 x 11   =   ☐
2 x 11   =   ☐
3 x 11   =   ☐
4 x 11   =   ☐
5 x 11   =   ☐
6 x 11   =   ☐
7 x 11   =   ☐
8 x 11   =   ☐
9 x 11   =   ☐
10 x 11  =   ☐
11 x 11  =   ☐
12 x 11  =   ☐

### 15) Division

99 ÷ 11   =   ☐
55 ÷ 11   =   ☐
11 ÷ 11   =   ☐
110 ÷ 11  =   ☐
66 ÷ 11   =   ☐
22 ÷ 11   =   ☐
121 ÷ 11  =   ☐
77 ÷ 11   =   ☐
33 ÷ 11   =   ☐
132 ÷ 11  =   ☐
88 ÷ 11   =   ☐
44 ÷ 11   =   ☐

Do you need help with the division exercise?

Remember: 4 x 11 = 44
So what will 44 ÷ 11 be?
Yes, that's right. It's 4!

Now your turn
11 x 8 = 88
16) 88 ÷ 11 = _____

Here is another one.
17) 12 x 11 = _____ (You should know this without singing as it is the last number on the 11 times table.)

18) 110 ÷ 11 = _____

30

Let us do one more. 9 x 11 = _____

19) 99 + 11 = _____

20) Fill in the missing numbers

11 ____ 33 ____ ____ 66 ____ 88 ____ 110 ____ ____

____ 22 ____ ____ 55 ____ ____ ____ 99 ____ ____ ____

21) Challenge: Mixed questions

10 x 11 = ☐
4 x 11 = ☐
6 x 11 = ☐
3 x 11 = ☐
8 x 11 = ☐
2 x 11 = ☐
11 x 11 = ☐

Some Division Challenge

(Use circles for this challenge, it will make it easier)

55 ÷ 11 = ☐
22 ÷ 11 = ☐
132 ÷ 11 = ☐
77 ÷ 11 = ☐
99 ÷ 11 = ☐
33 ÷ 11 = ☐
11 ÷ 11 = ☐

# Part B: Short division: Use the bus stop method

 Tip: Use the bus stop method for this exercise.

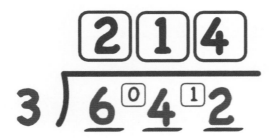

a)

6 ⟌5484

c)

3 ⟌900

e)

7⟌2415

b)

9 ⟌8523

d)

8 ⟌5944

f)

5⟌4535

# Chapter 5
# Part A: 12 Times table

 **Tip:** Sing the 12 times table song when doing this exercise.

**1) Multiplication**

| | |
|---|---|
| 1 x 12  = | |
| 2 x 12  = | |
| 3 x 12  = | |
| 4 x 12  = | |
| 5 x 12  = | |
| 6 x 12  = | |
| 7 x 12  = | |
| 8 x 12  = | |
| 9 x 12  = | |
| 10 x 12 = | |
| 11 x 12 = | |
| 12 x 12 = | |

**2) Division**

| | |
|---|---|
| 108 ÷ 12 = | |
| 60 ÷ 12  = | |
| 12 ÷ 12  = | |
| 120 ÷ 12 = | |
| 72 ÷ 12  = | |
| 24 ÷ 12  = | |
| 132 ÷ 12 = | |
| 84 ÷ 12  = | |
| 36 ÷ 12  = | |
| 144 ÷ 12 = | |
| 96 ÷ 12  = | |
| 48 ÷ 12  = | |

**3) Advanced challenge: Long multiplication**

carry stays

$4 \times 5 = 20$

+2  2  4
      3  5
   1  2  0
+  7  2  0  ← always put a
   8  4  0     place holder here

+1  2  4
         3
   7  2

a)
```
    2 2
  × 2 5
  -----
```

b)
```
    3 2
  × 2 7
  -----
```

c)
```
    4 1
  × 3 6
  -----
```

d)
```
    9 0
  × 7 2
  -----
```

e)
```
    8 1
  × 2 4
  -----
```

# Part B: Adding and subtracting fractions

 **Tip:** Use the Smile and Kiss method.

**Example and questions on fractions with common denominator.**

When adding and subtracting fractions, the first thing to check is if the denominators (bottom number) are the same.

If the denominators are the same, then it's pretty easy: just add or subtract the numerators (top number) and write the result over the same denominator.

$$\frac{3}{6} + \frac{2}{6} = \frac{5}{6}$$

$$\frac{2}{4} + \frac{3}{5} = \frac{10 + 12}{20} = \frac{22}{20} = 1\frac{2}{20} = 1\frac{1}{10}$$

smile

1) $\frac{1}{5} + \frac{2}{5} =$ _____ = _____

2) $\frac{2}{7} + \frac{3}{7} =$ _____ = _____

3) $\frac{2}{8} - \frac{5}{8} =$ _____ = _____

4) $\frac{3}{9} + \frac{4}{9} =$ _____ = _____

5) $\frac{1}{4} - \frac{2}{4} =$ _____ = _____

6) $\dfrac{1}{6} - \dfrac{3}{4} =$ _____ = ___

7) $\dfrac{3}{4} + \dfrac{4}{5} =$ _____ = ___

8) $\dfrac{4}{9} - \dfrac{1}{4} =$ _____ = ___

9) $\dfrac{3}{4} + \dfrac{5}{1} =$ _____ = ___

10) $\dfrac{7}{1} - \dfrac{4}{9} =$ _____ = ___

11) $\dfrac{1}{8} + \dfrac{3}{4} =$ _____ = ___

# Part C: Multiplying fractions

 **Tip:** Use the Zoom Zoom method.

Multiply the numerators: times the top numbers together Multiply the
denominators: times the bottom numbers together.

$$\xrightarrow{\text{Zoom Zoom}}$$

$$\frac{2}{5} \times \frac{1}{3} = \frac{2}{15}$$

$$\xrightarrow{\text{Zoom Zoom}}$$

1) $\dfrac{2}{4} \times \dfrac{3}{5}$ = ——— × ——— = ——

2) $\dfrac{7}{8} \times \dfrac{4}{5}$ = ——— × ——— = ——

3) $\dfrac{4}{9} \times \dfrac{3}{7}$ = ——— × ——— = ——

4) $\dfrac{8}{10} \times \dfrac{2}{9}$ = ——— × ——— = ——

5) $\dfrac{11}{15} \times \dfrac{4}{10}$ = ——— × ——— = ——

# Part D: Dividing fractions

 **Tip:** Use the **KFC** method (Keep, Flip, Change).

**Step 1:** Keep the first fraction.
**Step 2:** Flip the 2nd fraction.
**Step 3:** Change the division sign (÷) to a multiplication sign (x).

$$\frac{2}{3} \div \frac{5}{6} =$$

Keep    Change    Flip

$$\frac{2}{3} \times \frac{6}{5}$$

## Now Zoom Zoom

Zoom Zoom →

$$\frac{2}{3} \times \frac{6}{5} = \frac{12}{15} \begin{matrix} \div 3 \\ \div 3 \end{matrix} = \frac{4}{5}$$

← Zoom Zoom

Solve.

$$\frac{2}{4} \div \frac{3}{5} = \frac{2}{4} \times \frac{5}{3} = \frac{10}{12} \begin{matrix} \div 2 \\ \div 2 \end{matrix} = \frac{5}{6}$$

1) $\frac{2}{4} \div \frac{3}{4} = \underline{\phantom{x}} \times \underline{\phantom{x}} = \underline{\phantom{x}} = \underline{\phantom{x}}$

2) $\frac{7}{8} \div \frac{4}{5} = \underline{\phantom{x}} \times \underline{\phantom{x}} = \underline{\phantom{x}} = \underline{\phantom{x}}$

3) $\frac{4}{9} \div \frac{3}{7} = \underline{\phantom{x}} \times \underline{\phantom{x}} = \underline{\phantom{x}} = \underline{\phantom{x}}$

4) $\frac{8}{10} \div \frac{2}{9} = \underline{\phantom{x}} \times \underline{\phantom{x}} = \underline{\phantom{x}} = \underline{\phantom{x}}$

5) $\frac{11}{15} \div \frac{4}{10} = \underline{\phantom{x}} \times \underline{\phantom{x}} = \underline{\phantom{x}} = \underline{\phantom{x}}$

# Part E: Multiplying decimals with 10s, 100s, 1000s

**Multiplying**

**Steps**

- Move to the right once from the decimal point if multiplying by 10
- Move to the right 2 times from the decimal point if multiplying by 100
- Move to the right 3 times from the decimal point if multiplying by 1000 etc.

$$2.8341 \times 10 = 28.34$$

$$2.8341 \times 100 = 283.4$$

$$2.8341 \times 1000 = 2834.1$$

**Multiply.**

1) $6.7 \times 10 =$ _____

2) $7.523 \times 100 =$ _____

3) $26.2317 \times 1000 =$ _____

4) $445.16 \times 10 =$ _____

5) $8.911 \times 1000 =$ _____

6) $0.007234 \times 1000 =$ _____

# Part F: Dividing decimals with 10s, 100s, 1000s

**Dividing**

**Steps**

- Move to the LEFT once from the decimal point if dividing by 10
- Move to the LEFT 2 times from the decimal point if dividing by 100
- Move to the LEFT 3 times from the decimal point if dividing by 1000

**Divide.**

1) 6.7 ÷ 10 = _____

2) 7. 523 ÷ 100 = _____

3) 26. 2317 ÷ 1000 = _____

4) 445.16 ÷ 10 = _____

5) 8.911 ÷ 1000 = _____

6) 7234 ÷ 1000 = _____

# Part A: Recall all the Times tables

1 □    3 □    5    6 □    8 □    10    11 □

2 □    6 □    10    12 □    16 □    20 □    □

3    6 □    12 □    □    21 □    27 □    33 □

4 □    12 □    20 □    28 □    36 □    44 □

5 □    15    20 □    30 □    40 □    50 □    60

6 □    18    24 □    36 □    48 □    60    66 □

7 □    21 □    □    42 □    56 □    70 □    □

8 □    24 □    40 □    56 □    72 □    88 □

9 □    27 □    45    54 □    72 □    90 □    108

10 □    30    40 □    60 □    80 □    100 □    □

11 □    33 □    55    66 □    88    99 □    121 □

12 □    36 □    60    72    84 □    108 □    132 □

# Part B: Fraction of an amount

 Tip: Sing the fraction of an amount song.

**Step1:** Divide by the bottom.
**Step 2:** Times by the top

See an example below:

$\frac{2}{5}$ of 40

Step 1 : 40 divided by the denominator (bottom number)
$40 \div 5 = 8$

Step 2: Times your answer from step 1 by the numerator (top number)
$8 \times 2 = 10$

Solve

1. $\frac{1}{6}$ of 24 = _____    4. $\frac{5}{6}$ of 30 = _____

2. $\frac{7}{10}$ of 40 = _____    5. $\frac{1}{9}$ of 27 = _____

3. $\frac{1}{8}$ of 80 = _____    6. $\frac{3}{9}$ of 18 = _____

# Part C: Short division including decimals

Example

$$7.2 \div 3$$

$$\begin{array}{r} 2.4 \\ 3\overline{)7.\overset{1}{\underline{2}}} \end{array}$$

**Step 1:** How 3s many go into 7? = 2 remainder 1

**Step 2:** Put the 1 next to 2 to make 12. How many 3s in 12 is 4

Hint: Psst: Don't forget the decimal point.

Solve

1)  $2\overline{)6.2}$    3)  $3\overline{)2.43}$    5)  $3\overline{)18.6}$

2)  $4\overline{)9.6}$    4)  $5\overline{)12.5}$    6)  $2\overline{)7.04}$

# Part D: Word problems

Solve in your exercise book and fill in the answers.

1) If you need 6 carrots to make a cake, how many cakes can be made with 126 carrots?

_____

_____

_____

2) In the number 58470, the digit 4 in this number has a value of 400. What is the value of the digit 8?

_____

_____

_____

3) There are 360 cars in the car park $\frac{1}{2}$ are red. $\frac{2}{5}$ are green. The rest are silver. How many silver cars are there?

_____

_____

_____

4) I spend 34p on the bus fare on weekdays. How much do I spend in a week?

_____

_____

_____

# Part D: Fractions, Decimals and Percentages (FDP)

- Fraction of an Amount
- Fractions, Decimals and Percentages (FDP)
- Ordering FDP

# Part E: Fraction of an amount Song: Divide by the bottom, times by the top

A unit fraction is a fraction where the numerator is equal to 1. To find the unit fraction of a number, you need to divide the number by the denominator.

Example: To find $\frac{5}{6}$ of 24, we need to divide 24 by 6 which is 4. Then multiply 4 by 5 which is 20. Answer is 20.

1) Find the value of the fractions:

| Answer |
|---|
|  |
|  |
|  |
|  |
|  |

a) $\frac{1}{2}$ of 12 =

b) $\frac{1}{3}$ of 9 =

c) $\frac{2}{8}$ of 8 =

d) $\frac{2}{6}$ of 24 =

e) $\frac{3}{4}$ of 36 =

1) Circle the largest amount in each pair given:

a) $\frac{1}{4}$ of 32

b) $\frac{2}{3}$ of 33

c) $\frac{2}{5}$ of 25

d) $\frac{1}{3}$ of 27

e) $\frac{1}{5}$ of 100

f) $\frac{2}{5}$ of 30

# Part F: Fractions, Decimals and Percentages (FDP)

Question1 has been done for you, complete Questions 2 to 5 in Part B

|  | Fractions | Percentage | Answer Decimal |
|---|---|---|---|
| 1) | $\dfrac{2}{5}$ | × 20  $\dfrac{2}{5}$ = $\dfrac{40}{100}$  × 20 | Hint: To get the decimal, divide 40 by 100  0.40 |
| 2) | $\dfrac{1}{4}$ | $\dfrac{1}{4}$ = $\dfrac{?}{100}$ | |
| 3) | $\dfrac{3}{5}$ | = | |
| 4) | $\dfrac{2}{3}$ | = | |
| 5) | $\dfrac{6}{8}$  (Hint: simplify this fraction first) | = | |

49

# Part G: Ordering FDP

Hint with ordering FDP: Change all numbers to decimals or all to percentages first before you put in order.

First example has been done for you below, read through carefully, then attempt questions a to d

Example Question

| 0.61 | $\frac{2}{3}$ | 59% | 0.55 | $\frac{3}{5}$ |

Firstly, I will attempt to convert each of the figures above to percentages, lets take it one by one

0.61 → to convert to a percentage, just multiply by 100

0.61 x 100 = 61%

$\frac{2}{3}$ -> first convert this fraction to a percentage (see illustration of how below)

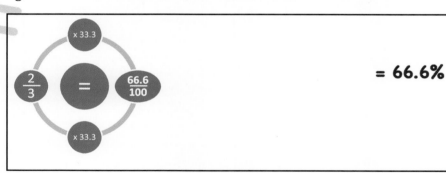

= 66.6%

59%                    Already a percentage, so no need to do anything

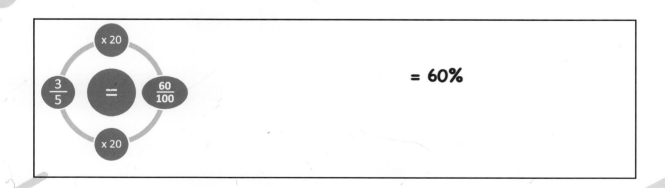

= 60%

50

0.55 to convert to a percentage, just multiply by 100

$$0.55 \times 100 = 55\%$$

Now that we have converted each one to percentages, let's put them in order.

| 0.61 | $\frac{2}{3}$ | 59% | 0.55 | $\frac{3}{5}$ |
|------|------|------|------|------|
| 61% | 66.6% | 59% | 55% | 60% |

Now it is easy to put in order (starting from the smallest)

| 0.55 | 59% | $\frac{3}{5}$ | 0.61 | 66.6% |

1) Now try these questions (starting from the smallest), get a piece of paper to map out your answers.

| a) | 81% | 0.78 | $\frac{4}{5}$ | $\frac{3}{4}$ | 0.805 |
|------|------|------|------|------|------|

| Answers | | | | | |
|------|------|------|------|------|------|

| b) | $\frac{1}{3}$ | 0.3 | $\frac{1}{4}$ | 28.5% | 0.32 |
|------|------|------|------|------|------|

| Answers | | | | | |
|------|------|------|------|------|------|

| c) | 0.23 | 21% | $\frac{1}{5}$ | $\frac{22}{100}$ | 19.2% |
|---|---|---|---|---|---|
| Answers | | | | | |

| d) | 1% | 0.012 | $\frac{3}{100}$ | 0.021 | $\frac{1}{40}$ |
|---|---|---|---|---|---|
| Answers | | | | | |

# Answers

## Chapter 1
### Part A: 1, 2 and 3 Timestable

1)

$1 \times 1 = 1$

$2 \times 1 = 2$

$3 \times 1 = 3$

$4 \times 1 = 4$

$5 \times 1 = 5$

$6 \times 1 = 6$

$7 \times 1 = 7$

$8 \times 1 = 8$

$9 \times 1 = 9$

$10 \times 1 = 10$

$11 \times 1 = 11$

$12 \times 1 = 12$

2)

$9 \div 1 = 9$

$5 \div 1 = 5$

$1 \div 1 = 1$

$10 \div 1 = 10$

$6 \div 1 = 6$

$2 \div 1 = 2$

$11 \div 1 = 11$

$7 \div 1 = 7$

$3 \div 1 = 3$

$12 \div 1 = 12$

$8 \div 1 = 8$

$4 \div 1 =$

3)

$1 \times 2 = 2$

$2 \times 2 = 4$

$3 \times 2 = 6$

$4 \times 2 = 8$

5 x 2  = 10
6 x 2  = 12
7 x 2  = 14
8 x  2 = 16
9 x 2 = 18
10 x  2 = 20
11 x 2  = 22
12 x 2  = 24

4)
18 ÷ 2 = 9
10 ÷ 2 = 5
2 ÷ 2 = 1
20 ÷ 2 = 10
12 ÷ 2 = 6
4 ÷ 2 = 2
22 ÷ 2 = 11
14 ÷ 2 = 7
6 ÷ 2 = 3
24 ÷ 2 = 12
16 ÷ 2 = 8
8 ÷ 2 = 4

5) 24 ÷ 2 = 12

6)
1 x 3 = 3
2 x 3 = 6
3 x 3 = 9
4 x 3 = 12
5 x 3  = 15
6 x 3  = 18
7 x 3  = 21
8 x  3 = 24
9 x 3  = 27
10 x 3 = 30
11 x 3  = 33
12 x 3  = 36

7)
$27 \div 3 = 9$
$15 \div 3 = 5$
$3 \div 3 = 1$
$30 \div 3 = 10$
$18 \div 3 = 6$
$6 \div 3 = 2$
$33 \div 3 = 11$
$21 \div 3 = 7$
$9 \div 3 = 3$
$36 \div 3 = 12$
$24 \div 3 = 8$
$12 \div 3 = 4$

8) $27 \div 3 = 9$

9) $30 \div 3 = 10$

10) Multiplication and division are linked with 3 numbers, because $3 \times 10 = 30$, therefore $30 \div 10 = 3$

11) Fill in the missing numbers

2   4   6   8   10   12   14   16      18   20    22 24

3   6   9   12   15 18   21   24   27   30   33 36

12) Challenge: Mixed Questions
$2 \times 3 = 6$
$4 \times 2 = 8$
$6 \times 3 = 18$
$5 \times 2 = 10$
$2 \times 1 = 2$
$9 \times 3 = 27$

Part B : Factors
1) Factors of 4: 1, 4, 2
2) Factors of 6: 1, 6, 2, 3
3) Factors of 12: 1, 12, 2, 6, 3, 4
4) Factors of 18: 1, 18, 2, 9, 3, 6
5) 5 , 7, 8 and 38

6) 1, 3, 7, 21
7) 1, 2 and 6
8) 6

## Part C: Multiples
Complete the Rhyme
1) Multiples mean multiply, Times what? Times table
2) Multiples of 1: 1, 2, 3, 4, 5
3) Multiples of 2: 2, 4, 6, 8, 10, 12, 14
4) Multiples of 3: 3, 6, 9, 12, 15, 18, 21, 24

## Part D
1) Complete this prime number song 2, 3, 5, 7, 11, 13
2) How many legs do prime numbers have? 2
3) Legs are Factors
4) Is 15 a Prime number? No
5) Is 1 a Prime number? No
6) Prime numbers between 1 and 20: 2, 3, 5, 7, 11, 13, 17, 19
7) Prime numbers between 20 and 30: 23, 29
8) 1
9) All Prime numbers are odd? No. 2 is the only even prime numbers
10) Is 1 a prime number? No. It only has 1 leg (1 factor)

# Chapter 2
## Part A: 4, 5 and 6 Timestable

1)
$1 \times 4 = 4$
$2 \times 4 = 8$
$3 \times 4 = 12$
$4 \times 4 = 16$
$5 \times 4 = 20$
$6 \times 4 = 24$
$7 \times 4 = 28$
$8 \times 4 = 32$
$9 \times 4 = 36$
$10 \times 4 = 40$

11 x 4 = 44
12 x 4 = 48

2)
36 ÷ 4 = 9
20 ÷ 4 = 5
4 ÷ 4 = 1
40 ÷ 4 = 10
24 ÷ 4 = 6
8 ÷ 4 = 2
44 ÷ 4 = 11
28 ÷ 4 = 7
12 ÷ 4 = 3
48 ÷ 4 = 12
32 ÷ 4 = 8
16  4 = 4

3) 28 ÷ 4 = 7
4) 48 ÷ 4 = 12
5) Multiplication and division are linked with 3 numbers, because 4 x 12 = 48, therefore 48 ÷ 12 = 4
6)

  4  8  12  16  20  24  28  32  40  44  48

  4  8  12  16  20  24  28  32  40  44 48


7) Challenge: Mixed questions

10 x 4 = 40
4 x 4 = 16
6 x 4 = 24
3 x 4 = 12
8 x 4 = 32
2 x 4 = 8
9 x 4 = 36

8)
1 x 5 = 5
2 x 5 = 10
3 x 5 = 15
4 x 5 = 20

5 x 5 = 25
6 x 5 = 30
7 x 5 = 35
8 x 5 = 40
9 x 5 = 45
10 x 5 = 50
11 x 5 = 55
12 x 5 = 60

9)
45 ÷ 5 = 9
25 ÷ 5 = 5
5 ÷ 5 = 1
50 ÷ 5 = 10
30 ÷ 5 = 6
10 ÷ 5 = 2
55 ÷ 5 = 11
35 ÷ 5 = 7
15 ÷ 5 = 3
60 ÷ 5 = 12
40 ÷ 5 = 8
20 ÷ 5 = 4

10) 20 ÷ 5 = 4
11) 30 ÷ 5 = 6
12) Multiplication and division are linked with 3 numbers, because
3 x 6 = 30, therefore 30 ÷ 5 = 6

13) Fill in the missing numbers
5. 10 15 20 25 30 35 40 45 50 55 60
5. 10 15 20 25 30 35 40 45 50 55 60

14) Challenge: Mixed Questions
10 x 5 = 50
4 x 5 = 20
6 x 5 = 30
3 x 5 = 15
8 x 5 = 40
2 x 5 = 10
9 x 5 = 45

15)

1 x 6 = 6
2 x 6 = 12
3 x 6 = 18
4 x 6 = 24
5 x 6 = 30
6 x 6 = 36
7 x 6 = 42
8 x 6 = 48
9 x 6 = 54
10 x  6 = 60
11 x 6 = 66
12 x  6 = 72

16)

54 ÷ 6 = 9
30 ÷ 6 = 5
6 ÷ 6 = 1
60 ÷ 6 = 10
36 ÷ 6 = 6
12 ÷ 6 = 2
66 ÷ 6 = 11
42 ÷ 6 = 7
18 ÷ 6 = 3
72 ÷ 6 = 12
48 ÷ 6 = 8
24 ÷ 6 = 4

17) 42 ÷ 6 = 7
18) 72 ÷ 6 = 12

19) Multiplication and division are linked with 3 numbers, because  12 x 6 = 72, therefore 72 ÷ 6 = 12

20)

| 6 | 12 | 18 | 24 | 30 | 36 | 42 | 48 | 54 | 60 | 66 | 72 |
|---|----|----|----|----|----|----|----|----|----|----|----|
| 6 | 12 | 18 | 24 | 30 | 36 | 42 | 48 | 54 | 60 | 66 | 72 |

21) Challenge: Mixed questions

$10 \times 6 = 60$

$4 \times 6 = 24$

$6 \times 6 = 36$

$3 \times 6 = 18$

$8 \times 6 = 48$

$2 \times 6 = 12$

$9 \times 6 = 54$

$30 \div 6 = 5$

$12 \div 6 = 2$

$42 \div 6 = 7$

$24 \div 6 = 4$

$54 \div 6 = 9$

$66 \div 6 = 11$

$6 \div 6 = 1$

$42 \div 6 = 7$

$18 \div 6 = 3$

$6 \div 6 = 1$

$36 \div 6 = 6$

$72 \div 6 = 12$

$66 \div 6 = 11$

$48 \div 6 = 8$

22)

a) $19 \times 6 = 114$

b) $15 \times 6 = 90$

c) $17 \times 6 = 102$

d) $18 \times 6 = 108$

e) $14 \times 6 = 84$

Part B: Short Division

1) $90 \div 5 = 18$

2) $405 \div 5 = 81$

3) $165 \div 3 = 55$

4) $192 \div 4 = 48$

5) $90 \div 3 = 30$

6) $246 \div 3 = 82$

# Chapter 3

## Part A: 7 and 8 Timestable

1)

$1 \times 7 = 7$
$2 \times 7 = 14$
$3 \times 7 = 21$
$4 \times 7 = 28$
$5 \times 7 = 35$
$6 \times 7 = 42$
$7 \times 7 = 49$
$8 \times 7 = 56$
$9 \times 7 = 63$
$10 \times 7 = 70$
$11 \times 7 = 72$
$12 \times 7 = 84$

2)
$63 \div 7 = 9$
$35 \div 7 = 5$
$7 \div 7 = 1$
$70 \div 7 = 10$
$42 \div 7 = 6$
$14 \div 7 = 2$
$77 \div 7 = 11$
$49 \div 7 = 7$
$21 \div 7 = 3$
$84 \div 7 = 12$
$56 \div 7 = 8$
$28 \div 7 = 4$

3) $63 \div 7 = 9$
4) $84 \div 7 = 12$
   $10 \times 7 = 70$

5) $70 \div 7 = 10$

6) Fill in the missing numbers

7  14  21  28  35  42  49  56  63  70  77 84
7  14  21  28  35  42  49  56  63  70  77 84

7)

10 x 7 = 70

4 x 7 = 28

6 x 7 = 42

3 x 7 = 21

8 x 7 = 56

2 x 7 = 14

11 x 7 = 77

8)

35 ÷ 7 = 5

14 ÷ 7 = 2

84 ÷ 7 = 12

56 ÷ 7 = 8

77 ÷ 7 = 11

84 ÷ 7 = 12

21 ÷ 7 = 3

9) 7   14   21   28 35   42   49   56   63   70   77 84

10)

a)  22 x 7 = 154

b) 32 x 7 = 224

c) 41 x 7 287

d) 90 x 7 = 630

e) 81 x 7 = 567

11)

1 x 8 = 8

2 x 8 = 16

3 x 8 = 24

4 x 8 = 32

5 x 8 = 40

6 x 8 = 48

7 x 8 = 56

8 x 8 = 64

9 x 8 = 72

10 x 8 = 80

$11 \times 8 = 88$

$12 \times 8 = 96$

12)

$72 \div 8 = 9$

$40 \div 8 = 5$

$8 \div 8 = 1$

$80 \div 8 = 10$

$48 \div 8 = 6$

$16 \div 8 = 2$

$88 \div 8 = 11$

$56 \div 8 = 7$

$24 \div 8 = 3$

$96 \div 8 = 12$

$64 \div 8 = 8$

$32 \div 8 = 4$

13)

a) $22 \times 18 = 396$

b) $32 \times 28 = 896$

c) $41 \times 48 = 1968$

d) $90 \times 38 = 3420$

e) $81 \times 58 = 4698$

Part B: Short Division

a) $847 \div 11 = 77$

b) $261 \div 3 = 87$

c) $93 \div 1 = 93$

d) $64 \div 4 = 16$

e) $430 \div 5 = 86$

f) $588 \div 12 = 49$

# Chapter 4

Part A: 9, 10 and 11 Timestable

1)

$1 \times 9 = 9$

$2 \times 9 = 18$

$3 \times 9 = 27$

$4 \times 9 = 36$

5 x 9 = 45
6 x 9 = 54
7 x 9 = 63
8 x 9 = 72
9 x 9 = 81
10 x 9 = 90
11 x 9 = 99
12 x 9 = 108

2)
81 ÷ 9 = 9
45 ÷ 9 = 5
9 ÷ 9 = 1
90 ÷ 9 = 10
54 ÷ 9 = 6
18 ÷ 9 = 2
99 ÷ 9 = 11
63 ÷ 9 = 7
27 ÷ 9 = 3
108 ÷ 9 = 12
72 ÷ 9 = 8
36 ÷ 9 = 4

3)
72 ÷ 9 = 8
12 x 9 = 108

4)
108 ÷ 9 = 12
10 x 9 = 90

5) 90 ÷ 9 = 10

6) Fill in the missing numbers

9  18  27  36  45  54  63  72 81 90 99 108
9  18  27  36  45  54  63  72 81 90 99 108

7) Challenged: Mixed questions
10 x 9 = 90

64

4 x 9 = 36
6 x 9 = 54
3 x 9 = 27
8 x 9 = 72
2 x 9 = 18
11 x 9 = 99

45 ÷ 9 = 5
18 ÷ 9 = 2
108 ÷ 9 = 12
63 ÷ 9 = 7
99 ÷ 9 = 11
27 ÷ 9 = 3
9 ÷ 9 = 1

9)
81 ÷ 9 = 9
72 ÷ 9 = 8
90 ÷ 9 = 10
9 ÷ 9 = 1
18 ÷ 9 = 2
27 ÷ 9 = 3
10)
9  18  27  36  45  54  63  72  81  90  99  108

11)
1 x 10 = 10
2 x 10 = 20
3 x 10 = 30
4 x 10 = 40
5 x 10 = 50
6 x 10 = 60
7 x 10 = 70
8 x 10 = 80
9 x 10 = 90
10 x 10 = 100
11 x 10 = 110
12 x 10 = 120

12)

90 ÷ 10 = 9
50 ÷ 10 = 5
10 ÷ 10 = 1
100 ÷ 10 = 10
60 ÷ 10 = 6
20 ÷ 10 = 2
110 ÷ 10 = 11
70 ÷ 10 = 7
30 ÷ 10 = 3
120 ÷ 10 = 12
80 ÷ 10 = 8
40 ÷ 10 = 4

13)

a) 22 x 17 = 374
b) 32 x 27 = 864
c) 41 x 47 = 1927
d) 9– x 37 = 3330
e) 81 x 57 = 4617

14)

1 x 11 = 11
2 x 11 = 22
3 x 11 = 33
4 x 11 = 44
5 x 11 = 55
6 x 11 = 66
7 x 11 = 77
8 x 11 = 88
9 x 11 = 99
10 x 11 = 110
11 x 11 = 121
12 x 11 = 132

15)

99 ÷ 11 = 9
55 ÷ 11 = 5
11 ÷ 11 = 1

110 ÷ 11 = 10
66 ÷ 11 = 6
22 ÷ 11 = 2
121 ÷ 11 = 11
77 ÷ 11 = 7
33 ÷ 11 = 3
132 ÷ 11 = 12
88 ÷ 11 = 8
44 ÷ 11 = 4

**Part B: Short Division**

a)  5484 ÷ 6 = 914

b)  8523 ÷ 9 = 947

c)  900 ÷ 3 = 300

d)  5944 ÷ 8 = 743

e)  2415 ÷ 7 = 345

f)  4535 ÷ 5 = 907

# Chapter 5

**Part A: 12 Times table**
1)
1 × 12 = 12
2 × 12 = 24
3 × 12 = 36
4 × 12 = 48
5 × 12 = 60
6 × 12 = 72
7 × 12 = 84
8 × 12 = 96
9 × 12 = 108
10 × 12 = 120
11 × 12 = 132
45 × 12 = 144


2)
108 ÷ 12 = 9
60 ÷ 12 = 5
12 ÷ 12 = 1
120 ÷ 12 = 10
72 ÷ 12 = 6

$24 \div 12 = 2$
$132 \div 12 = 11$
$84 \div 12 = 7$
$36 \div 12 = 3$
$144 \div 12 = 12$
$96 \div 12 = 8$
$48 \div 12 = 4$

3)

a) $22 \times 25 = 550$

a) $32 \times 27 = 864$

b) $41 \times 36 = 1476$

c) $90 \times 72 = 6480$

d) $81 \times 24 = 1944$

## Part B: Adding and subtracting fractions

1) $3/5$

2) $5/7$

3) $3/8$

4) $7/9$

5) $1/4$

6) $7/12$

7) $31/20 = 1\ 11/20$

8) $7/36$

9) $23/4 = 5\ 3/3$

10) $59/9 = 6\ 5/9$

11) $7/8$

## Part C: Multiplying Fractions

1) $6/20 = 3/10$

2) $28/40 = 7/10$

3) $12/63 = 4/31$

4) $16/90 = 8/45$

5) $44/150 = 22/75$

**Part D: Dividing Fractions**

1) $2/3$

2) $35/32 = 1\,3/32$

3) $28/27 = 1\,1/27$

4) $18/5 = 3\,3/5$

5) $11/6 = 1\,5/6$

**Part E**
**Multiply**

1) 67

2) 752.3

3) 26231.7

4) 4451.6

5) 8911

6) 7.234

**Part F**
**Divide**

1) 0.67

2) 0.07523

3) 0.0262317

4) 44.516

5) 0.008911

6) 7.234

# Chapter 6

## Part A: Recall all the Timestable

```
1  2  3  4  5  6  7  8  9  10  11  12
2  4  6  8  10  12  14  16  18  20  22  24
3  6  9  12  15  18  21  24  27  30  33  36
4  8  12  16  20  24  28  32  36  40  44  48
5  10  15  20  25  30  35  40  45  50  55  60
6  12  18  24  30  36  42  48  54  60  66  72
7  14  21  28  35  42  49  56  63  70  77  84
8  16  24  32  40  48  56  64  72  80  88  96
9  18  27  36  45  54  63  72  84  90  99  108
10  20  30  40  50  60  70  80  90  100  110  120
11  22  33  44  55  66  77  88  99  110  121  132
12  24  36  48  60  72  84  96  108  120  132  144
```

## Part B:
1) 4
2) 28
3) 10
4) 25
5) 3
6) 9

## Part C : Short division including decimals
1) 3.1
2) 2.4
3) 0.81
4) 2.5
5) 6.2
6) 3.52

## Part D: Word Problems
1) 21 cakes
2) 8000
3) 36
4) £1.70

## Part E
1a) 6
1b) 3
1c) 2

1d) 8

1e) 27

2) b

*Part F*

1) 0.40

2) 0.25

3) 0.60

4) 0.66

5) 0.75

*Part G.*

1a) ¾, 0.78. 4/5, 0.805, 81%,

1b) ¼, 28.5%, 0.3, 0.32, 1/3,

1c) 19.2%, 1/5, 21%, 22/100, 0.23,

1d) 1%, 0.012, 0.021, 1/40, 3/100

## Our Story

Tecnis Academy began out of my interest in teaching children and supporting them to develop their confidence in their academic work.

Tecnis Academy started as a one person team with me visiting students homes to provide 1-1 tuition, this often involved driving from one house to the other with my then baby daughter (Now 9 years old) strapped on my back. At one point, I was visiting 20 homes in a week. In 2016, I decided to invite all my students to a small office space that I rented.

We grew from a small office to 4 centres across Kent, then COVID pandemic hit. Tecnis Academy moved all tuition services to virtual tuition during the pandemic and we have not looked back since then. Tecnis Academy now helps to improve learning for over 2000 students across 10 countries and we work hard to improve the quality of our students' learning experience every day. We provide regular free webinars and Live Talks offering Parents advice on the UK Educational System and Processes as well as free tips and tricks to help our students become high achievers in their academics.

For more information on our courses from pre-school through to A level covering Maths, English, Sciences, Reading, Writing as well as other subjects and our other services please visit tecnisacademy.com to find out more.

Tecnis Books are available via Amazon or via contactus@tecnisacademy.com (UK only)

Pre order now for £19.99

Offer available until 30<sup>th</sup> September 2023

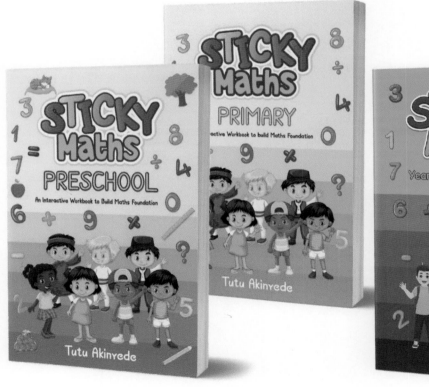

Printed in Great Britain
by Amazon

47482182R00046